STICKERS AGAINST THE PATRIARCHY

Skittledog

GIRL BOSS
EQUAL PAY

LIBERTÉ, EGALITÉ, SORORITÉ
Feminist AF
DON'T MANSPLAIN ME

SHE GETS
SHIT
DONE

GIRLS UNITE
DESTROY THE PATRIARCHY

LOUD, PROUD
POWERFUL
WOMAN
UP
LOVE

GRL PWR
HELLO I AM A
FEMINIST
ONE STRONG WOMAN
SHE DID THAT
FEMINIST
GIRL POWER

LET'S GO GIRLS

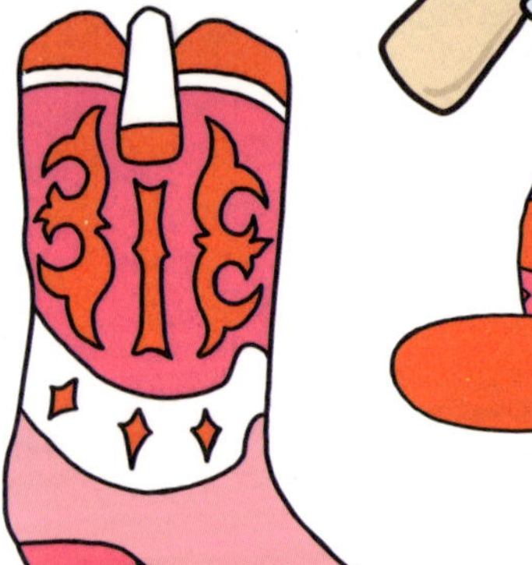

I FEEL LIKE
A WOMAN

NO1

WINNER

LIGHTS, CAMERA,
LIBERATION
TAKE 11/11

FEMME
LIBRE
QUEEN

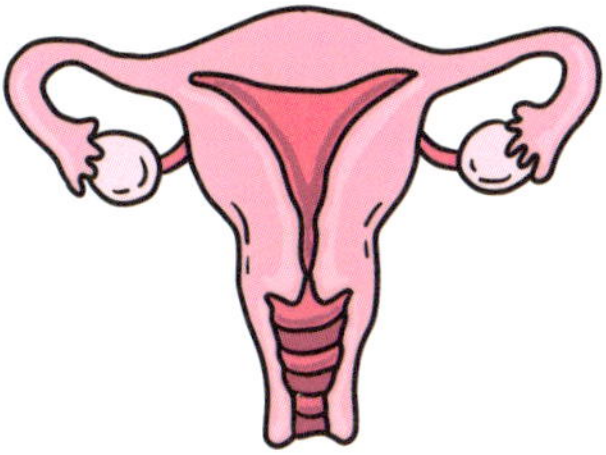

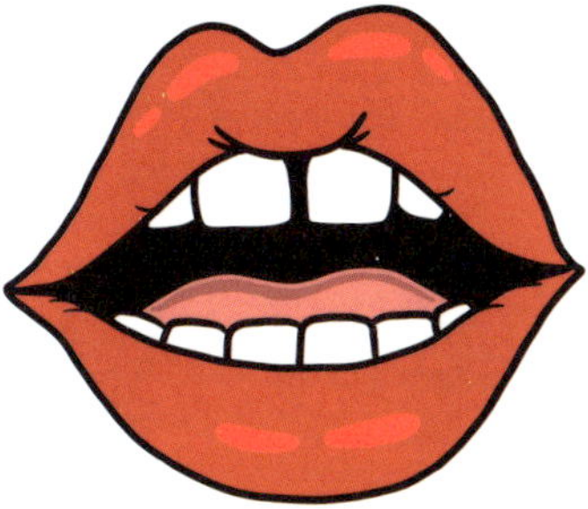

BIG
GIRL
PANTS

WOMEN'S
RIGHTS

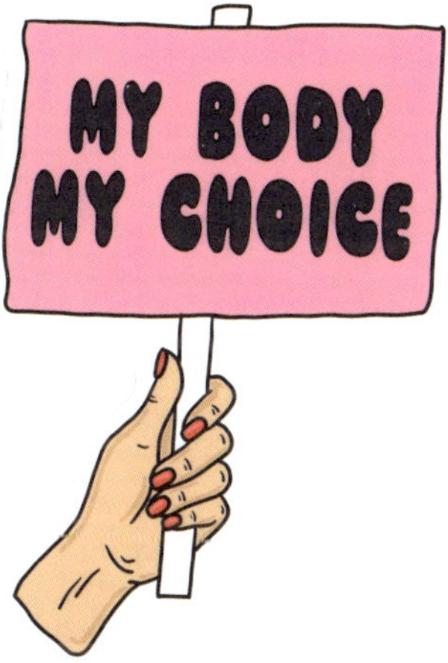
MY BODY
MY CHOICE

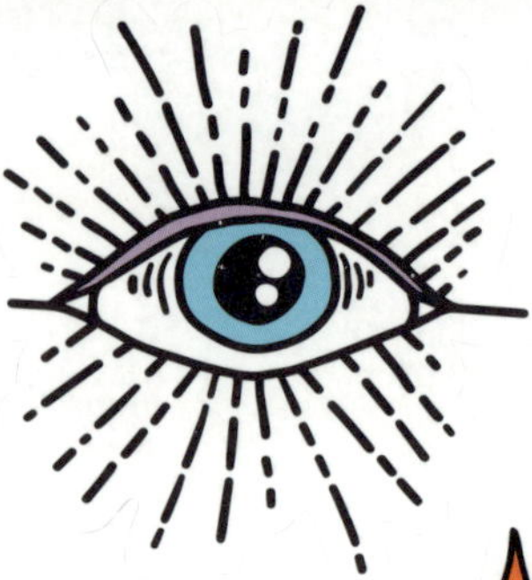

THE EMPRESS

PATRIARCHY
A BAD HANDBOOK

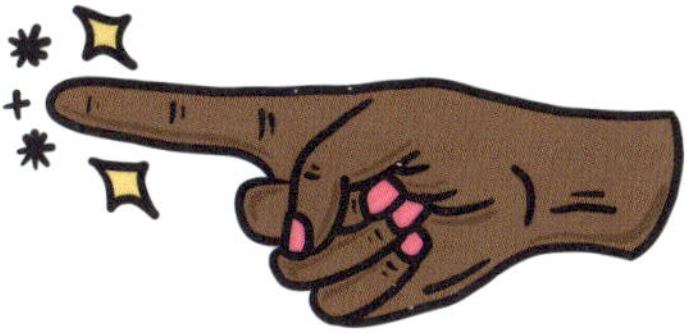

PATRIARCHY
POTION

RIP
GENDER ROLES
PATRIARCHY
FRAGILE EGO
INEQUALITY
MISOGYNY

PATRIARCHY
SAYS NO

PRO CHOICE
STICKERS AGAINST THE PATRIARCHY
UNSTOPPABLE

BAD
BITCH

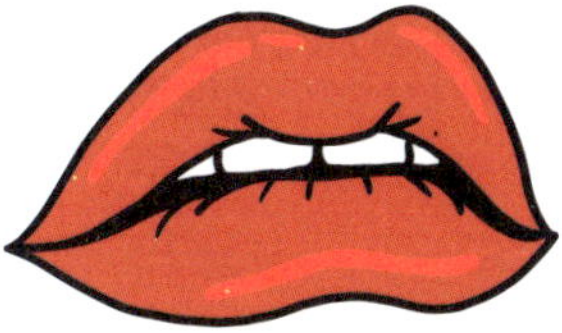

AGAINST
THE
PATRIARCHY

GIRL ON A MISSION

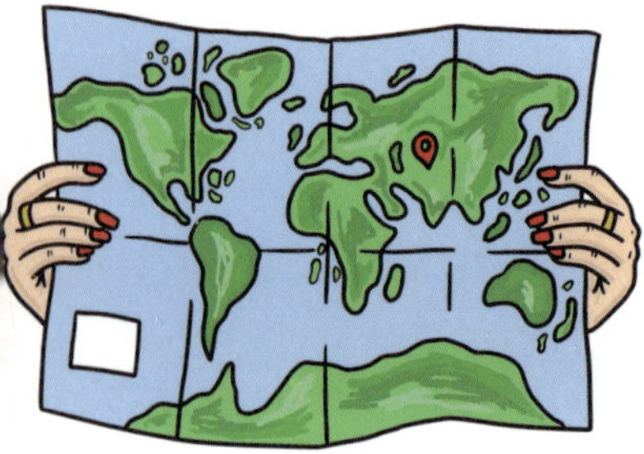

N
W
E
S

WE RUN THIS WORLD

FEMINIST

DO IT
NOW IS A GOOD TIME
YOU CAN
THIS IS YOUR SIGN

100
VOTE
GIRL MATH
OUTSPOKEN

VOICE
POWER
CHANGE
YOU
ARE
BAD
ASS

Skittledog

First published in the United Kingdom in 2026
by Skittledog, an imprint of Thames & Hudson Ltd,
6–24 Britannia Street, London WC1X 9JD

Designer: Alison Guile
Production: Felicity Awdry

EU Authorized Representative: Interart S.A.R.L.
19 rue Charles Auray, 93500 Pantin, Paris, France
productsafety@thameshudson.co.uk
www.interart.fr

A CIP catalogue record for this book is available from the British Library

ISBN 978-1-83776-118-0
01

Printed and bound in China by Starlite

FSC
www.fsc.org
MIX
Paper | Supporting responsible forestry
FSC® C122384

Be the first to know about our new releases, exclusive content and author events by visiting:

thamesandhudson.com
thamesandhudsonusa.com
thamesandhudson.com.au